Are There Any Minions In The House?

Monica D. Lloyd

Love Clones Publishing
www.lcpublishing.net

Copyright © 2015 by Monica Lloyd. All rights reserved. This book or any portion thereof may not be reproduced or used in any manner whatsoever without the express written permission of the publisher except for the use of brief quotations in a book review.

Printed in the United States of America

First Printing, 2015

ISBN: 978-0692596913

King James Version Scripture quotations marked "KJV" are taken from the Holy Bible, King James Version (Public Domain).

Publishers:
Love Clones Publishing
Dallas, TX 75205
www.lcpublishing.net

HONOR

I honor all those in all sectors of employment who work in a field providing service to humanity and the public. You did it. For this, you deserve the greatest of recognition.

Acknowledgement

Acknowledgement is the ability to recognize the existence of something in your life that can be addressed in either a positive or a negative connotation. It will depend on the individual from whom the acknowledgement comes if it is worth the time. Therefore, I have only one thing that I want to bring to the forefront that helped me to write this book, PEOPLE.

Life has taught me that no matter where you go people will be there. Knowing yourself and how you operate will bring fruitfulness in your relationships with them. People cannot be ignored, pushed aside, or placed on invisibility. They are here to stay and you have to learn how to deal with them. Since you didn't create them, you can't wish them away.

I acknowledge that I need people in my life. As much as I like to think I am a loner and enjoy being alone, it's a lie that I have collaborated within my own consciousness. I have somehow convinced myself that if I have no dealings with people they will have no reason to want to talk to me. WRONG!

Humanity is a species that was designed to connect with one another on purpose by the creator. Without going much into detail, Genesis 2:18 states-, *"And the Lord God said, It is not good that the man should be alone; I will make him an help meet for him."* If it's not good for a man, it cannot be good for a woman. In other words, we need each other. There is a song by Barbara Streisand which says, "People who need people are the luckiest people in the world", and she was right.

Special Thanks to:

Leaders, Co-Workers, Siblings, Bank Teller, Grocery Store Clerk, Laundromat Attendant, Tele Marketer, Mortgage Holder, Utility Personnel and a host of other people with whom I have to communicate on a daily basis. You make my servitude climb higher every day of my life. Providing good service is not only to be done in the church; it is anytime we have to connect ourselves with people.

Let us do better in serving others.

TABLE OF CONTENTS

Introduction
8

Chapter One
Boss versus Leader
16

Chapter Two
Following before Serving
21

Chapter Three
Appointed to Serve A Villain?
31

Chapter Four
If You Happy and You a Know It Clap Your Hands
38

Chapter Five
Mastering Your Position
44

Chapter Six
The Love of the Leader for the Servant
57

Chapter Seven
Start Over
67

Practice Makes Perfect 30 Days

INTRODUCTION

The movie "Despicable Me" has caught the attention of children and adults alike who are willing to display their young hearts. I know every time I hear the song, "*Happy"* by Pharell Williams, I begin to twist and move body parts that I thought were no longer movable. The characters in the story tell a plot that no matter how difficult things may be in your life, it could change in an instant. One minute you are fatherless and the next, someone adopts you as their own, loves you unconditionally and all that they possess now belongs to you.

The adopted children in this movie are loved unconditionally, free to enjoy their newfound life and the ability to dream without fear. Life is looking bright through the eyes of the ones who had lost hope.

This concept has been proven effective for many and remains an avenue of reach in order to have the laughter of children in ones' home. Children are a gift from God regardless if birthed or adopted.

The dictionary defines the word *despicable* means "someone who deserves to be hated and despised". These individuals don't feel worthy of anyone's love. Somehow life has beaten them down so horribly that bad decisions have frozen them in the past, setting them in a place of regret. They are unable to move forward having bitterness from the taste of today's disappointments and expectations of a future presenting the same, thereby locking them away from the world.

I like the word, "PAST". It lets me know, IT NO LONGER EXISTS. The good, bad or ugly is all gone. I cannot fix it, correct it, or hang on to it. I must move forward and live life to the fullest. I cannot allow it to breathe into me the corrupt decaying of its existence. It's gone and I must free myself by forgiving myself.

Villains were not born villains; circumstances in life changed the makeup of what could have been to accepting what is. Never except where you are! As the world turns on its axis daily your life can change in a day, a minute or a second. Many have not developed into what the creator intended, because you cannot see beyond your feet. Expand your vision, even if it has to start in your mind. See it there first until you can see it with your eyes, second.

Gru was the "unsuccessful" villain who wanted to shrink the moon. I never knew why villains always undertook what always appeared to be the unreachable. However, one must admire the tenacity they possessed in obtaining the goal of always wanting to RULE THE WORLD. Why, to be able to control what has hurt them and to make sure this pain will never happen again.

Here is the story line according to Universal Studios:

"In a happy suburban neighborhood surrounded by white picket fences with flowering rose bushes, sits a black house with a dead lawn. Unbeknownst to the neighbors, hidden beneath this home is a vast secret hideout. Surrounded by a small army of minions, we discover Gru, planning the biggest heist in the history of the world. He is going to steal the moon. (Yes, the moon!) Gru delights in all things wicked. Armed with his arsenal of shrink rays, freeze rays, and battle-ready vehicles for land and air, he vanquishes all who stand in his way. Until the day he encounters the immense will of three little orphaned girls who look at him and see something that no one else has ever seen: a potential Dad. The world's greatest villain has just met his greatest challenge: three little girls named Margo, Edith and Agnes.

-Written by Universal Pictures

"The world's greatest villain has just met his match". This is absolutely a thought provoking line. Have you ran into anyone and found out YOU HAVE MET YOUR MATCH? Of course, you have and they challenged you in every way possible by making you uncomfortable. Yes, you have met them and yet you knew you needed them. They were to be a part of your destiny as you travel down the road of life. Rather you like it or not your match is making you into a better YOU.

Gru ran into three little girls who will change his life forever. They didn't see a villain; they saw possibilities and hope of being unleashed from a prison of loneliness and despair. A place they knew well in the orphanage. No, he was not a villain, but a Father, someone who would accept them and love all three of them unconditionally. Gru had not a clue what was in these little girls mind. He was being set up for a new encounter with life and a new lifestyle. God does it just like that.

In "Despicable Me" there were these yellow organisms known as Minions whose sole purpose was to serve their master. They were of no use if they could not serve. Serving others is an art form that one can make into a masterpiece. There is no consideration of self when serving others. The Minions enjoyed their assignment to Gru; in so much that they observed him and thought ahead of what their master may need. Pleasing him at times was challenging, but attainable.

Serving any human being is going to be challenging; good days, bad days, unpredictable days, sick days, mood swing days, don't want to be bothered kind of days and just because days are sure to arise. The server must keep in the forefront of their minds, **DONT TAKE IT PERSONAL** your master is only human, and they are not God. If you can place this on a plaque somewhere for your viewing you will not get side tracked in your service. Be like the Minions, disappear or get quiet for the moment gather yourself, but do return. Don't be M.I.A.

"Are There Any Minions In The House?" is applicable to every kind of house that is in existence today; a place where people reside for a function of purpose. This could be your place of employment, your sanctuary, your home or even dorms where students live for their college experiences. Every house must have order and every house must have Minions (Servers). If you do not, I can guarantee that your house is in utter chaos. Not only do you need leaders, there must be servers.

There is a story in the bible where the Apostles were teaching the word of God and this required a lot of their time. The multiplying of the people brought on some complaining and murmuring about the widows being overlooked in the distribution of food. Read what occurred:

"In those days when the number of disciples was increasing, the Hellenistic Jews among them complained against the Hebraic Jews because their widows were being overlooked in the daily distribution of food. So the Twelve gathered all the disciples together and said, "It would not be right for us to neglect the ministry of the word of God in order to wait on tables. Brothers and sisters, choose seven men from among you who are known to be full of the Spirit and wisdom. We will turn this responsibility over to them and will give our attention to prayer and the ministry of the word." This proposal pleased the whole group. They chose Stephen, a man full of

faith and of the Holy Spirit; also Philip, Procorus, Nicanor, Timon, Parmenas, and Nicolas from Antioch, a convert to Judaism. They presented these men to the apostles, who prayed and laid their hands on them." Acts 6:1-6

Here the Leaders were attentive to the assignment at hand; that being The Word. No attention was given to what the people (well in this case, the widows) were missing out on, until someone took notice of the disputes. The solution to the problem was SERVERS. The Apostles told the people, "You pick seven men" and their requirement must be full of the spirit and wisdom. There are two important Kingdom aspects in serving. In your home or place of employment it could be something else, but whatever it is, the solution to the disputes are servers. Leaders cannot do it alone. There are other matters to which attention must be given. The Apostles set the rules and requirement and the people did the picking of the individuals to whom they trusted to do the job. Afterwards, they brought them unto the apostles to lay their hands on them. Problem solved.

This is a good lesson for leaders. Allow your people to pick out who is capable of carrying out what you have **ordered**, not you. Establish the requirements and goals and let the people work it, not you. Your order has been placed, now go back to the matters at hand.

As you continue to read this book, take notice of the Servant and Leader relationship and how it can develop into something grand for both parties. Leaders allow your vision to be broadened to see through the eyes of the one that is serving, and to the server allow me to show you your leader. I guarantee after reading, "Are There Any Minions In The House" it will bring productivity with outstanding hospitality to any Business and Church.

Having served leaders of all capacities for years has taught me, it's not about me, but what can I provide for you as the solution. It is called, customer service. Enjoy the contents and enjoy the better you that will come forth as you prepare to be more effective in your service.

Chapter One
Boss versus Leader

I started working at the age of sixteen through the work program at my high school. My first place of employment was a nursing home being a certified nursing assistant (CNA). The title has changed over the years, but the tasks and responsibilities have remained the same. I continued my education from CNA to a Licensed Practical Nurse (LPN) to Registered Nurse (RN), which my patients called becoming a 'Real Nurse'. The statement was humorous in nature, but it showed a growth process.

In each role I occupied, I encountered different managers along the way; some good, bad, and ugly with a wealth of knowledge. Lessons learned would not be easily forgotten. The observation of these individuals made it clear to me the kind of style I would perform if ever I came into a position of this magnitude. This is not to say all my experiences were negative, just purposeful for my building.

While in high school during my senior year, I came to know Christ as my Lord and Savior. My life changed drastically. Coming from a Pentecostal background, much of my school activities ceased. The leader of the church I attended expressed concerns of my spiritual growth if I continued in certain endeavors. Therefore, removing myself from the current clubs, I chose to mature in the knowledge of a God.

Over the years, I learned what I participated in was not a sin, but would become a distraction in the plans of God for my life. My leader was concerned about my soul prospering as well as my relationship with Christ.

Often times we acknowledge we have Supervisors at work and Leaders at church. The same way I expressed my two scenarios above. Why do you never hear people say, *my leader at work* or *my supervisor at church?* Is it the norm that supervisors work and leaders lead? There are times it is noticed that the roles are reversed. You may have a terrific leader at work and a supervisor at church.

I recall times when I have said, "I have no boss, but God". Yet God is not even a boss, He is a Leader. Knowing the difference between the two will help you better serve your gift. It is your gift that brings you before important people. Serve them well.

The Boss Characteristics
Do as I say, not as I do mentally.

This is why you are dictated your orders; do this, do that, complete this, complete that without any examples set before you. You are trained to be seen and not heard. This is why bosses never want to hear your input. There is no team concept. In knowing this you will not frustrate yourself when you cannot verbalize.

This kind of leading has produced people who are insecure, intimidated, and unable to think ahead. Whatever fruit is brought forth is not worth eating. Robots are made instead of thinkers. The servants have been programmed to perform without thought.

No vision is cast before the people. No outcomes established. Focus is on results. It is like an assembly line with the results being a device that no one understands how it works.

The Leader Characteristics

Let US go and do this and do that, complete this and that then says, *Follow Me*.

Leaders are Initiators. They show their people the way, because the vision is in the leader and the followers must understand execution of the vision or it will not come to pass. Remember the childhood game, *Follow the Leader?* You did what you saw your leader do; jump on one foot, turn around in circle all while watching who was in front showing the way.

Jesus told two men after they finished fishing, **"Follow Me and I will make you fishers of men"** in Matthew 4:19. Leaders provide the vision and it will be totally your choice if you wish to follow.

The best moral of any company comes from when you a have a leader that is able to pull its people together and allow them to be a part of the process. The concept of WE made this happen flows through, not only the leader, but also the workers. High morals produce great results. Bosses are selfish and glory seekers. It is all about them while credit is taken.

In this season, leaders are needed and because of the daunting of the vision, servants are required to help the vision happen. Consider yourself well qualified to serve a leader or manager when called upon. Let no one remove you from that place. The distinction between the two should not affect how service should be provided only the manner in which one carries themselves. Remaining obedient and loving is the acceptable mode of action.

Servants are created Leaders in the making.

Chapter Two
Following before Serving

I have had only four places of employment since the age of sixteen. I did not practice jumping from one place to another. My tenure at each place seemed to be ten years. My season of change was winter and by the month of November, I would find myself at a new place. This occurred three times.

While employed, I made sure that I followed all procedures and policies given to me in order to pass my probationary period. Once those ninety-days were completed, it allowed me the opportunity to show forth the knowledge that was invested within me.

Following requires observing without speaking. A tenacious task for some, but you must understand that it is needful. I can remember one of my trainers stating that she would not answer any questions until all was completed. You were to write your questions on the paper she provided. I thought "How rude". By the end of the session, I had ten questions and drew lines through all ten. Why? Because during her presentation she answered every single question on my paper as she continued to explain, what was needed out of us as new employees. Following her instructions, while noticing key points, spared me much embarrassment. Places of employment are very good in making followers while serving.

Probationary means *the testing and trial of one's conduct.* During this period, you are being observed in:

- Attitude
    - The way you answer questions.
    - Gestures
- Appearance
    - Cleanliness of uniforms (Are they wrinkle free?)
- Ability to follow commands
    - Follow through with No back talking.
- Team Work
    - Not being standoffish. Participating in the group.
- Timeliness
    - Manage time by being ahead of time.

All these qualities are essential, in addition to a host of other qualities. It is imperative that you display the best you if you want the job. Ninety-Days is a long time to pretend to be someone you are not. The real you is bound to show up.

Let us say you passed the probationary period, and you have secured the job. How are you going to make their investment profitable? Time and cost went into training you. No employer is expecting you to fail. They are looking for a profit. Your ability to manifest your training in a superior way will depend on you getting the opportunity to serve in a greater way. Pay attention to whom you are following, for it will tell you where you are going.

The Story About Investment

"It's also like a man going off on an extended trip. He called his servants together and delegated responsibilities. To one he gave five thousand dollars, to another two thousand, to a third one thousand, depending on their abilities. Then he left. Right off, the first servant went to work and doubled his master's investment. The second did the same. But the man with the single thousand dug a hole and carefully buried his master's money.

"After a long absence, the master of those three servants came back and settled up with them. The one given five thousand dollars showed him how he had doubled his investment. His master commended him: 'Good work! You did your job well. From now on be my partner.' "The servant with the two thousand showed how he also had doubled his master's investment. His master commended him: 'Good work! You did your job well. From now on be my partner.' "The servant given one thousand said, 'Master, I know you have high standards and hate careless ways, that you demand the best and make no allowances for error. I was afraid I might disappoint you, so I found a good hiding place and secured your money. Here it is, safe and sound down to the last cent.' "The master was furious. 'That's a terrible way to live! It's criminal to live cautiously like that! If you knew I was after the best, why did you do less than the least? The least you could have done would have been to invest the sum with the bankers, where at least I would have gotten a little interest. "'Take the thousand and give it to the one who risked the most. And get rid of this "play-it-safe" *who won't go out on a limb. Throw him out into utter darkness.'* Matthew 25:14-30 (MSG)

This man was placing his money into SERVANTS hands, not enemies. He knew their abilities and gave unto them what he knew they could handle. How do we know this? From understanding the meaning of the word 'Ability'. To know one's ability you have to be familiar with the capacity in which they can hold and this can only be known by following or being followed. He knew these servants. He knew their proclivities, weaknesses and strengths. He did not give them all the same amount; he gave them different amounts for different abilities. Some of you have developed $5,000 abilities, $2,000 abilities and others $1,000 abilities, but the key is "You have an ability." Work it!

In following trust is accrued. Growth begins to happen as a relationship is formed. You are learning how the one you follow do business, communicate, respond to requests, and remain quiet even when you think they should speak. You are being allowed to see a side of them that is seldom seen by others. Following is a privilege that is not appreciated by many and misunderstood by viewers. You cannot let anyone talk you out of following the one assigned to you, for if you do; a great opportunity will be forfeited by your hands.

Here it is, the Master of the house is going on a trip and has entrusted some (not all) of his money to three servants. Sure, he had more, but he saw potential in these three. He delegated responsibility and placed authority upon them to act as he would act with his own money. Then he left.

Sidebar: *Following brings with it an anointing to become a representative of the one who sent you. –The same authority and rights are placed in your hands. What an awesome privilege.*

Immediately two of the servants went working, but working where? They are servants, doing business as they have observed their master doing business. Taking chances as they saw their master take chances, investing as they saw their master invest, and buying stock as they saw their master buy stock. Whatever they saw their master do, they did. Now can you understand when Jesus parents found him and expressed how worried they were, Jesus informed them "I must be about my Father's Business"? Jesus knew there was no time to waste; business is at hand.

These two servants most likely entered the circles where their master had previously traveled and taken them. Why not? They had full right to negotiate as they had observed him do on many occasions. They knew the language for they observed his speech. They dressed the part for they observed his style. The servants were confident in what they had acquired of their master and had no problem displaying it. They were business minded. Doubling profit is good from any angle at which you look whether is $5,000 to $10,000 / $2,000 to $4,000. No one could be disappointed in that.

The third servant went and buried his $1,000.00. No attempt was made to try anything. Do you think he was following purposefully? It does not appear to be. You do yourself an injustice if you are following and only take heed to the negative parts of serving. No employer only wants to hear what you don't like about the job; share what you like also. What improvements can you bring to the establishment? Are you intuitive? The servant put no forethought to do anything with what was placed in his hands.

After a long journey the man of the house returns. A business meeting was held and each servant had to present his or her portfolio. The one who had $5,000 showed his master how he doubled what entrusted to him and the same with the one who had $2000. The master replies to the both of them, "Good work! You did your job well. From now on be my *Partner'*. WOW!

They were no longer servants, but partners. The servants get to share in all the excitement of his world. The now ex-servants are capable of handling their own businesses. They advanced from following, to serving, into partnership. This is a great accomplishment with honor attached. A good leader is one who can place purpose in servants' hands, watch and see what comes into fruition, then elevate them. The master did not tell them what to do with the money. He only saw their abilities. He delegated responsibilities, which means anointed them to represent in his absence. As a leader, are you able to release and let your people do what you have invested in them?

The servant that buried his ability to handle $1,000 lost his previous position to serve. If you are unable to produce what was invested in you while following, your service will no longer be required. You Are Fired!

Think about your place of employment. If you do not become progressive in the position assigned unto you, it will be given to another. Promotions are always on the horizon for servants who work well. You may consider it overwhelming when you are given another's responsibilities and think it is not fair, but it's a compliment. The master took the $1,000 previously given and gave it to the first one who doubled his investment, because potential of success was favored upon him. Because of your newfound position, you will delegate responsibilities to those whom you see abilities in as well.

Following builds endurance during the journey. If you are able to keep up there are prepared places being designed for your arrival. Do not take for granted the 'call' to come is because no one else could fulfill the assignment. You will be deceiving yourself. Leaders call those whom they know are capable of handling the task, but also who are willing vessels. Are you willing to follow? Then answer the call and follow the commands.

Remove these consecutive five words from your vocabulary, 'I Can Not Do That'. In saying this, you have already fixed your outcome. The servant given $1,000 not only failed his master, but failed himself. His point of view was distorted. Any profit is considered profit regardless if it is 1% or 10%. The energy it took to find a place to hide the money could have been utilized to invest the money. Use your energy wisely.

Trainers play a key role in your performance or success. These investors of the company are so viable to the maintaining of the new employees. They may be called preceptors or role models. They were chosen to show you the ropes of the establishment due to their great performance and understanding of the vision. This is an honor, but seldom viewed as extra work. Poor mind set can be viewed as burying $1,000. Having the potential, but not wanting to do the work.

CHAPTER THREE
Appointed to Serve A Villain?

Gru is known as a Villain; one who is hated and despised. Do you know of any villains, or should I say, someone you have categorized as a villain? Do they exist, or is it their character is detrimental to the server? Either way you have been appointed to serve them. Congratulations!

While employed at a certain establishment some time ago, I had the hardest time working under a leader who was different from any manager I have ever encountered. In my eyesight she was unreasonable and a predator of the weak. One day I met a colleague of my manager who knew her from time past at my church home, I was introduced to her by my pastor. Once the visitor found out I was a nurse, she asked where I worked, and somehow the mentioning of my manager's name brought this response, "Oh I know her. She is so ARCHAIC in her thinking and style of leadership". I was like, that makes sense, Archaic or primitive of thought.

Serving someone who rubs you the wrong way is not an excuse for not fulfilling assignments. All leadership styles need servants that will serve unconditionally, with the agape love of God flowing through them.

Over the years of servitude from Corporate America to the Pulpit, I have learned there are no villain leaders, only individuals who are misunderstood due to their own past and personal failures that spill over into their business or spiritual life. It is not as it seems to appear. Take a step back, look at your leader and look within. With the reputation of being a villain, as I stated earlier was not always considered the case. Something in life caused a change to come.

Before I left that establishment, progression and promotion was my portion. The manager and I was a great team. We became good working *partners*. I took the time to learn her while building a trusting environment that was not competitive. I was not a threat, but became a colleague.

You may never get to this status with your leader and you have to be content in knowing this. They may never see you being valuable, but it does not decrease your self-worth. Continue to serve them for it is building character in you, so that when your time comes to be the leader you will know how NOT to act. Be courteous and responsive without attitude. Allow your demeanor to be pleasant. It will get to a point that your presence will be comforting to those you serve in the midst of their chaotic world.

You Were Chosen to Serve... You Are Hired!

A leader is equipped to seeing potential and abilities within their employees. A resume plays a major role in showing the perspective hirer your accomplishments while displaying your talents. It is imperative that you keep your resumes updated for there will come a time when you will be called upon. This is why resume classes in conjunction with how to interview seminars are offered to those who want to improve their chances of being hired.

King Saul saw a perspective candidate that had abilities he wanted to possess in his business. His name was David, the baby son of Jesse. David wasn't looking for a job. His father sent him with lunch to feed his brothers who worked for the king. The time was getting late; they were doing a lot of overtime. Jesse wanted to make sure his boys were eating and getting along all right (just like a parent).

Upon arrival, David immediately noticed something was wrong. Why was everyone standing around looking defeated, afraid as if to be frozen in time? Then it happened, the tall loud speaking man came out proclaiming how he was going to do a hostile takeover. Every remaining employee will be his slave as he rules over them relentlessly. The contender name was Goliath.

According to the dictionary, Goliath is described as a very large, powerful, or influential person. These kinds of individuals can be quite frightening, especially if you are looking up from where you are. Intimidation is a tool of warfare that is often used. Once you allow your mind to see yourself defeated, you are. King Saul with his men saw themselves becoming slaves with no recourse of survival. There was no way of an escape, The Company was at its end.

A strong indignation arose up in David. Goliath has threatened a company that has been around for generations to generations. It was the company that has kept his family from ruin, allowing them to live a fruitful life since he could remember. It is an honorable company with the establishmentarian being a God fearing man that knows justice and equality. This cannot be. It would not be if David could help it.

Sidebar: Anytime you are the answer to the problem, expect enemies from within.

The brothers of David ridiculed him. Tantalizing him to mind his own business and that he was too young to do anything. What the brothers forgot is their baby brother is a server who has observed how the master works. David recalls the conversations at the kitchen table that his family had about business or the ins and outs of dealing with people. Be creative in your strategies. Never allow your opponent see what your right hand is doing. He took mental notes as it was discussed how to act in the presence of your enemies. Never let them see you sweat. He may not have punched the clock, but he understood the duties.

David dismissed the criticism. Someone took notice of David's enthusiasm and reported it to King Saul. The King repeated to David what he had already heard from the others, but this time David presented his resume:

David said to Saul, "Your servant was tending his father's sheep. When a lion or a bear came and took a lamb out of the flock, I went out after it and attacked it and rescued the lamb from its mouth; and when it rose up against me, I seized it by its whiskers and struck and killed it. Your servant has killed both the lion and the bear; and this uncircumcised Philistine will be like one of them, since he has taunted and defied the armies of the living God." David said, "The Lord who rescued me from the paw of the lion and from the paw of the bear, He will rescue me from the hand of this Philistine." And Saul said to David, "Go, and may the Lord be with you."

1 Samuel 17:34-37 AMP

Saul said, "Go, and may the Lord be with you!" David was hired on the spot. This was a young man who was not looking for a job, but the leader had need of him. He was appointed to serve. David was triumphant in overcoming Goliath and keeping the business from being dispersed. No employees lost. Saul was very impressed with David. A position was made for him to reside from that day, no more unemployment. (1 Samuel 18:2)

There will be leaders who will challenge you to become a better you. They are not villains. You must not view them as such, for if you do the impartation that is required for your appointment to serve will not come into fruition. You can learn something from every manager, director, pastor, teacher, leader whom you serve and to whom you find yourself connected. However, you must be receptive and teachable. Changing your attitude will bring elevation.

The minions in the movie 'Despicable Me' did not care that Gru was a villain for they were designed to serve anybody. You too are appointed to serve ANYBODY! Someone is waiting to hire you, but are you willing to be challenged? Only you can answer this question. I have often heard a co-laborer say, what they cannot take and will not take, but keep showing up every day. No matter how bad you interpret your management, you keep showing up with a smile. Why? For you know you need the money. Therefore, you keep providing the service needed until you can find another leader to follow. It is a rotating cycle. You have just proven you are gifted to serve anyone. Grasp it and be productive in it. As like David, You Are Hired.

CHAPTER FOUR
If You Happy and You Know It Clap Your Hands

As I watched the minion's movie in the theater, there was a multiplicity of personalities on display. No two seem to be the same. These little yellow organisms were always laughing. They laughed at themselves as they laughed at each other, and played jokes on one another while they got each other out of trouble. It was simply enjoyable to watch. Serving was fun for them. They were happy.

Mentees are called butt kissers, Armor Bearers/Adjutants are called flunkies, and Special Assistants are despised. There is no respect for servitude. It makes those who provide it feel unappreciated due to those who do not comprehend its purpose and are being judgmental in their thinking. These individuals, "servants" are purposely designed to help someone's journey become easier in travel.

I see caddies do it for golfers in the hot sun for hours. They are patient, calm, and calculative in their movements with their golfers they have been appointed. It is as if they are watching to see what could be done to help make the shot be successful. There should be no complaining about how hot it is or how long the hours are just pure observation on the assignment at hand.

A caddie is the person who carries a player's bag and clubs, and gives insightful advice and moral support. A good caddy is aware of the challenges and obstacles of the golf course being played, along with the best strategy in playing it. This includes knowing overall yardage, pin placements and club selection.

wikipedia.org/wiki/Caddy

Sidebar: *Servants are never concerned with what they need, only with what is needed for the server.*

Learning to enjoy what you do goes beyond watching whom you serve. It should be the job that is exciting. It is accomplishing the goal that creates exuberance within your soul. Your happiness cannot be based on people, for if it does, you have already failed. People are not perfect and neither are you.

Mistakes will be made and excuses given, but servitude must continue.

I recall taking care of a Dementia patient on the unit I worked. While changing him, this male patient literally slapped me so hard that my glasses flew from my face unto the floor, not once, but twice. I didn't retaliate, and I did not verbally abuse him. As I was cleaning my glasses in the bathroom that I picked up from off the floor, I overheard one of the nursing assistants who was with me exclaim, "He slapped the sh$# out of her," Drying the tears from my eyes and cleaning my face I came out and stated, "Yes he did, but notice; I did not hit him back. The day any of you hit him, you will be fired".

Leaders go through some internal turmoil that you know nothing about and you may be hit in the crossfire. Yes, it hurts. No, it does not feel good. Yes, you may want to cuss, but you can't. Learn to remove yourself in order to get yourself together. It is allowed.

The clapping of hands is the showing forth of appreciation. Appreciation is the provision of recognition. Recognition is the identification or acknowledgement of achievement. "If you happy and you know it clap your hands" is saying you appreciate the recognition of your own achievements that are displayed from within. You are happy because you know you have done well, good and faithful servant and no one can take that away from you.

I was very pleased with my reaction when my patient slapped me. My growth and development showed. I realized I am rooted and grounded in God to provide good customer service at any cost, even if it hurts me. It may cost me shame, being belittled, or scrutinized, but that is nothing compared to failing at my assignment. Failure is not an option.

One of the greatest members of the human body are the hands. Hands can heal with a touch or cause harm. Hands can give away something or take it back. Hands can bring comfort or pain. The choice is up to you. Don't allow your hands to become the source of dishonesty to your leaders. The moment there is distrust displayed through your hands, your service to them is over. Skepticism sets in and idle thoughts of your servitude moves to the forefront of their minds. Your hands are no longer considered a source of comfort. The Lord wants clean hands and a pure heart before Him (Psalms 24:4) and your leaders require the same.

One of the five senses is touch. A touch can bring healing to the body and soul without saying any words. It is known as nonverbal communication. Have you ever been lost for words to say to make a situation better for someone? All of a sudden, you reached out to touch them by a rubbing of the hands, hug, kiss or sit close to the individual and just breathe together. Sometimes words will bring confusion, whereas a touch is softly spoken words without sound. Both servant and leader can grow in this area without feeling that all circumstances need a fix. Maybe silence is the answer.

The most used body part in servitude are your hands; to carry, pour, lift, open, close, plug in, clean, drive and so on. Very seldom is your voice heard, but your stature is recognizable. Get out of position and watch your leader. The eye contact alone can cut you up. One thing a businessperson does not like to do is look for their staff. They need to be on point. Psalms 23 states, "THE STAFF COMFORTS ME" which means they guide and keep focus. I am speaking metaphorically, but it's true for within your hands lay the plans. The one you serving hands are usually freed up to shake hands with others.

Clap your hands and realize how important they are. Think yourself happy, and you will be happy. Reevaluate why you do what you do. Be gentler with your hands. Make your hands become more fruitful and intentional in movement. They are your greatest asset.

CHAPTER FIVE
Mastering Your Position

One has to learn how to master any position that is held. Rather in politics, a board room, emergency room, or an attendant in the bathroom. Whatever position you occupy, mastering it is the key to your success. No Jacks-Of-All-Trades need to apply, only those who are willing to master their skill.

The problem is that people have never been trained in their positions. The titles have been given with no roles and responsibilities provided. People are making it up as they go and are failing miserably. There has to be a major overhaul done in this area across the globe.

Potential has been seen in these individuals, but no mentors have stepped up to train them through the process. Instead, everyone feels that they have arrived. Arrived where, I must ask? A title does not automatically place one in the position of performance; it has given direction for travel.

The course has been set to move from one level to another with productivity being the result of the training because of understanding. Servants produce what has been learned without fear, and leaders have to distinguish between laziness versus fear. Fear breeds uncertainty with movement, whereas laziness brings idleness with procrastination and very little (if any) movement. The servant that buried what his master gave him MOVED in fear to bury it, but he moved. The problem was that he used his energy against himself instead of for himself.

It took time, thought, and muscle to find the right place to dig a hole and bury the money, so that thieves would not come and steal it. This servant had great potential, but could not see it in himself. He was not lazy; he was insecure (Matthew 25).

In mastering your position there will be mistakes that should cause a determination within you to better execute your performance if you desire it. Anything placed in your hands by your leader is an indication that you can handle it, so handle it. Work it until you cannot work it anymore to its lowest denominator.

In your serving, you cannot be concerned with how others may view you. People will literally talk you out of your position because of their insecurities. Be confident and know that you are called for such a time as this, to serve. Be not deceived by what you hear or see. Someone is waiting on you not to complete your assignment so that he or she can take your position. A position taken was a position not filled. Therefore, stay put.

C.U.P. Your Position

C ~ Control
U ~ Use
P ~ Perform

By using these keys, you will become successful in your servitude.

Control

Mastering your position is having the ability to restrain yourself. Control your emotions. Control your motives. Control your mouth. Control your environment. This list is endless. The main theme is you must know your strengths and weaknesses. What gets under your skin? What can send you off? You must know these things and control them. Never allow them to flare up in public places. It will diminish your servitude in the eyesight of others.

I often hear people say, "I can't help myself". What you are saying is "I have no control". What comes up comes out with no regards to the consequences. You are not mastering your position in this behavior. It is a bad representation and you speak as a child, which may require you to sit for a season until further growth is developed. As an employee, your superiors often do not want to hear what you have to say. Controlling your tongue will keep you in the room, whereas speaking too much will get you dismissed.

A Mistress and her Servant Leader ~ Sarai and Hagar

Genesis 16:1-9 Amp

Now Sarai, Abram's wife, had not borne him any children, and she had an Egyptian maid whose name was Hagar. So Sarai said to Abram, "See here, the Lord has prevented me from bearing children. I am asking you to go in to the bed of my maid so that she may bear you a child; perhaps I will obtain children by her." And Abram listened to Sarai and did as she said. After Abram had lived in the land of Canaan ten years, Abram's wife Sarai took Hagar the Egyptian maid, and gave her to her husband Abram to be his secondary wife. He went in to the bed of Hagar, and she conceived; and when she realized that she had conceived, <u>she looked with contempt on her mistress regarding Sarai as insignificant because of her infertility</u>. Then Sarai said to Abram, "May the responsibility for the wrong done to me by the arrogant behavior of Hagar be upon you. I gave my maid into your arms, and when she realized that she had conceived, I was despised and looked on with disrespect. May the Lord judge who has done right between you and me." But Abram said to Sarai, "Look, your maid is entirely in your hands and subject to your authority; do as you please with her." So Sarai treated her harshly and humiliated her, and Hagar fled from her. But the Angel of the Lord found her by a spring of water in the wilderness, on the road to Egypt by way of Shur. And He said, "Hagar, Sarai's maid, where did you come from and where are you going?" And she said, "I am running away from my mistress Sarai." The Angel of the Lord said to her, "Go back to your mistress, and submit humbly to her authority." *Genesis 16:1-9 (AMP)*

Contempt toward your superiors can be seen as well as heard. Once you view the one you have been appointed to serve as beneath you, your removal is inevitable. Hagar (the servant) thought of herself more highly than she should due to the fact she was able to give her leader's husband what she could not, a child. She had no control in her demeanor. Therefore, the repercussion was too hard for her to bear, and she ran away.

Running away was not the solution. Instead, humility was needed, and God indicated such. Hagar had to return to Sarai and learn again how to "submit humbly to her authority". God allows second chances in servitude for there is purpose in it. If you follow long enough you, (the server) will get pregnant either with a vision, calling, promotion, ministry etcetera that will come into fruition, and you need your leader's help to bring it forth. Stay in position and control yourself.

I am privileged often to follow my leaders to assignments in which they are called in order to serve them. I do not make it my assignment by passing business cards or getting in their conversations. I make sure my leader is comfortable and I move my body away enough so I can see them and they can see me just in case anything is needed. I am at their constant disposal. I watch my body posture, facial expressions, my words, and my tongue. I make it my business not to embarrass my leaders; I am in control. Hagar had become an embarrassment to Sarai. Sarai trusted her with her husband and a promised seed.

Sidebar: Your leaders will trust you with their secrets if you have control.

Use

Applying the talents and/or gifting you possess to be employed or utilized by someone is usage. There are people who are in need of you and looking for you. Employers use your skills every time you work and pay you for it. Your gift has made room for you and brought you before great men (Proverbs 18:16).

The problem is you do not know your gift nor understand how to market yourself. I am the last one to discuss marketing, but I can say, I do allow the usage of my gifts; some with pay, and some by the use of my time. For in the servitude of my gift, doors open in order for my gift to be expanded into places I never would have been able to tread upon on my own accord.

Leaders make room for those who serve them, especially if they are proud and secure of your development. It shows the impartation/training has taken root. Do not step ahead of them, but keep in step with them.

Have you ever heard, "If you don't use it, you will lose it"? For example, if you do not speak Spanish daily it will become dormant and not easily accessible when needed. I didn't say it was gone, I said, dormant. Meaning it is there, but you have to wake it up in order to USE it again.

In mastering your position, be proactive. You do not always have to be asked to do, just do. A cup holds things. It is designed for that purpose. You never have to ask a cup, "Can I Use You?" It is on the shelf waiting to be picked up and utilized. The watching and observing of your leaders leads you to do things ahead of time. Have the coffee ready, the files ready, messages on the desk, computer on, pencils sharpen, whatever it is you observed they USE on a daily basis, have it ready. They will appreciate it more than you will ever know. No one can get mad with anyone for USING his or her brain.

Perform

There is a movie I love titled, The Karate Kid. There have been multiple versions of it, but the storyline remains the same. A mother moves with her son to a place suitable for the both of them. The son is bullied and falls into the caring hands of a man that can teach him karate techniques that will make living where they are a little easier as he learns control, use and performance.

The training starts out with menial chores that are believed by the young man that he is the elder man's slave. Frustration sets in until it is explained that the actions helped build defensive blocks through muscle memory while also learning personal balance of spirit and body. In other words, Karate techniques were being taught all the time and there came a time when he had to perform. (Wikepedia.org/karate kid)

Do not despise small beginnings. Cleaning bathrooms and toilets may seem degrading, but it is teaching humility. Not being recognized for your accomplishments is teaching you not to get hooked on the praises of men. The lack of being appreciated without receiving "Thank you" or "Please" is teaching know your own self-worth. Your muscles are being built. It's called, menial chores and your character is being put to the test before you perform. Before David ever fought a giant, he had to conquer a lion and a bear. Not for his sake, but for the safety of the sheep he was assigned to protect. (1st Samuel 17:34)

Past experiences builds confidence to moral excellence with insight and understanding, which brings with it self-control and exactness of knowing what needs to be accomplished by loving those you serve. You were being prepared all the time, like David. You will be held accountable to protect those whom you serve from your own laziness, back biting, envy, jealousy, high mindedness before you ever protect them from others. You have to learn "Personal Balance" for a life could depend on it.

In mastering your position through performance, learn to be ready at all times. You may not know when your leader will call upon you to perform your gift. You must report for duty, especially if promotion is behind the call. David performed by killing Goliath and promoted to stay with King Saul, never to return home. Leaders love to have people around them who can perform with power.

The bible says, "The greatest among you is a servant" and that can be anywhere, the White House or your house. If you know how to serve, you are a great Man or Woman. The President of the United States goes nowhere without servants. Competent men and women are there to perform at every request. CEOs have Administrative Teams within his/her reach. The Five Fold ministry of God have Armor Bearers/Adjutants for their servitude. Performers are needed everywhere, so my question is this, "Are There Any Minions In The House?" for you are needed.

Never be afraid to execute and bring into fruition what you have been trained to do. Do it in style. Bishop T.D. Jakes says it this way, Maximize the Moment. Make them remember you when you are no longer standing there. The Karate Kid won the tournament through all the pain. He pushed through it. Push yourself through all the naysayers and their negative comments concerning your service. What they are not aware of is this; you are serving to become a Partner later. Continue the journey.

C.U.P. your assignment and Hold your position. You are about to be picked up.

Vision

No business will be productive or fruitful if it remains "top heavy". All leaders with no Minions will fail. There has to be feet to any vision that is put into place.

> *"Write the vision and engrave it plainly on clay tablets, so that the one who reads it will* **run**. *"For the vision is yet for the appointed future time. It hurries toward the goal of fulfillment; it will not fail. Even though it delays, wait patiently for it, because it will certainly come; it will not delay.*
>
> *Habakkuk 2:2-3 AMP*

Vision provides the runners with direction after reading what was put into place. It is the responsibility of the visionary to make sure that every single line is understood. Servers can only discern or comprehend the assignment to a certain degree. The establishmentarians, if they want a successful business, will meet and greet their staff as often as needed to hear and see if the runners are clear of the goal. The bible says the vision *"Hurries toward the goal of fulfillment"*. Runners are anxious. They are pacing in step. All they are waiting on is the word, GO, but go where?

Minions (Servers) are missing in the house. The mind-set has to be renewed about servitude. It is not a dirty job, but an honorable position. I often tell people, if a leader asks you to do anything do not refuse for it is building your muscles, confidence and your endurance. The tasks are leading to greatness. It could be from the bathroom to the mailroom to the boardroom who knows, but if you cannot do the menial work, you will not do well with more responsibility being placed upon you.

Vision yourself beyond where you are now. Be the visionary of your life and run. Businesses come into fruition because the person learned how to master their position and work the plan. As you serve, pick up your hand full of purpose that is left behind and know you are not forgotten, for a reward awaits you for your servitude.

CHAPTER SIX
The Love of the Leader for the Servant

In the previous chapters, much was said about the Minion to Leader relationship and how this can develop into something very productive. Not only does the servant serve, but also if done well the leader will reciprocate the same unto the servant.

"Now a Roman centurion's slave, who was highly regarded by him, was sick and on the verge of death. When the centurion heard about Jesus, he sent some Jewish elders to Him, asking Him to come and save the life of his slave. When they reached Jesus, they pleaded with Him earnestly to come, saying, "He is worthy for you to do this for him, because he loves our nation and he built us our synagogue at his own expense." And Jesus went with them. But when He was near the house, the centurion sent friends to Him, saying, "Lord, do not trouble yourself further, for I am not worthy for you to come under my roof. Therefore I did not even consider myself worthy to come to you. But just speak a word, and my slave

will be healed. For I also am a man subject to authority, with soldiers under me; and I say to this one, 'Go,' and he goes, and to another, 'Come,' and he comes, and to my slave, 'Do this,' and he does it." Now when Jesus heard this, He was amazed at him, and turned and said to the crowd that was following Him, "I say to you, not even in Israel have I found such great faith as this man's." When the messengers who had been sent returned to the house, they found the slave in good health."

Luke 7:2-10 AMP

Here was a Commander of an army over multiple men who had deep respect and concern for one of his men. Someone he viewed as being valuable to him.

Sidebar: ***If you are seen valuable to your leader, there is absolutely nothing they will not do for your wellbeing, even sacrifice their reputation.***

The centurion had a good reputation with other leaders of the land. He was a philanthropist that sowed seeds for the betterment of the community and was held in high esteem by other rulers. He sent them to Jesus to make a request known for his servant and it was these rulers that convinced Jesus to show up. You must understand that this is remarkable. The bible says they were Jewish Elders coming on the behalf of a Roman Soldier, to speak to Jesus about a servant; a slave that people regarded as useless. The curiosity of it all amazed Jesus enough to just show up and meet this man of influence.

As Jesus got closer to the house the centurion sent yet out another servant to inform Him he did not have to come into the house, just speak a word and the servant would be healed. Why would he have Jesus come all this way, but not let him in the house? The Commander knew that having Jesus in the proximity of the location would bring change with his words, for he too was a man of authority and those whom he was over obeyed his words. The centurion heard of Jesus reputation and the outstanding healing he has done. This stopped Jesus in his tracks. Did an about face to address the crowd about this man's faith.

A Leader of Influence

Your leader has the ability to open doors and present brand new opportunities along the way, because of the love they have toward you and the service you have provide them. It is not in vain. When you serve without an interior motive, you will be rewarded openly. Benefits start coming your way. Unexpected blessings show up at your door. Bonuses are shared with regard to your service.

Great leadership is the ability to utilize influence to help others. What Business Men/Women know is that high moral produces results. When people feel appreciated, not tolerated; they will give you the best of themselves without a charge. The centurion's servant did that for him. His leader wanted him well and healthy.

I recall something in my life when I became ill. This process went for about three months before I could find out what was actually wrong with me. I continued to work while being sick at the same time. You could see the changes taken place within me for I dropped a surmountable amount of weight and I saw the concern on my co-workers and church member faces.

One day the illness became too much to bear, and my body began to break down at my place of employment. My supervisor was my centurion. She was, "Johnny on the spot." I laugh now thinking about it. She rolled me to the Emergency Department, had the staff take me to a room immediately. She called my personal physician to inform him of my status and stayed with me until things were not so critical. I knew then, I had been serving well. No one will take that much time out for a servant who does nothing but mumble and complain. She may not have called for the Elders, but she handled what she could. I am thankful for her.

A Leader of Resources

A leader has resources for their people. These resources can get one to their next level of elevation. Their knowledge comes from experiences that can be stepping-stones for their followers. They are not selfish or self-centered for they know it takes a team to move the vision forward.

Resources are supplies that can be drawn upon when needed. True leaders must never misuse or take advantage of these resources. When this happens the Servants will not be effective in fulfilling vision if the leaders do not release the resources. The centurion knew people in high places in which to call and get a favor. He used his resources so that his servant could be healed. He did not hold back his hand and let the man suffer just to prove a lesson. He made phone calls and expected a return.

A Leader of Humility

The centurion had to be a man that understood you catch more bees with honey than vinegar. Some leaders are very demanding. They can appear to people very demeaning and full of pride. This character flaw can be a turn off and cause people to follow with resentment.

The bible says that he sent the Jewish leaders to "Ask Him to come" which means it wasn't a guarantee that he would. He humbled himself to save the life of another, which is the mark of a great leader. Colossians 4:1 states, *"Masters, deal with your slaves justly and fairly, knowing that you also have a*

Master in heaven". Every leader should have a leader for it brings forth accountability.

He considered (thought about his own life and decided) that he was not deserving of Jesus to come into his house. How awesome is that! People forever want to display the things they have; homes, cars, jewelry, money, etcetera, to the point that it is worn on their bodies daily. This man says, just speak the word and all will be well for I know words have authority. Here is humility at its best. The centurion and his servant shows what a relationship can become without any hindrances, with each being truthful to their respective roles. When you love people, it does not matter what title you hold, only the service rendered.

Here was a man who knew how to go low. He has authority, coming under authority, so that the authority of another man will bless someone he loves. It was not for the centurion's benefit, but for the benefit of his servant. It didn't bother him if it would cause shame or embarrassment. He is a businessman and risks must be taken in order for him to be successful.

Leaders bring Results

One of the many qualities of a leader is fruitfulness. Having the ability to build from nothing to something shows forth imagery in action and it all started out with an idea. That is why it is good to THINK: to have a conscious mind of something particular as the subject of your mind. For as a man think of himself, so shall he become and manifest in the world.

Leaders are thinkers. If you can think it, you can obtain it. All you have to do is pursue after it. The word 'NO' is not comprehended well in the mind of a leader. This word brings too much finality when there is always a way, even if it has to be created. The centurion knew this and operated in opportunities that will bring results to the words he spoke. He was a man of authority who recognized a man in a realm of authority that he did not possess, but knew how to make his request known.

You may not have all the knowledge, but you know people who do and pulling on their gift will help you accomplish your goal. Surrounding yourself with people who know more than you, are abilities that can be used along the journey, while developing networks of value. Never become jealous of your counterparts. Knowing those who labor among you is what a great leader learns. If you cannot find what you need in your circle, it is time to go out of your circle and seek for what is needed and the centurion did exactly that. "When the messengers who had been sent returned to the house, they found the slave in good health." RESULTS manifested.

Once again, your leaders love you and are appreciative of what you do for them even if it may not be sated of words. Action speaks louder than words (I have been told), so watch and observe your leader's action. I guarantee they are speaking very loudly.

Providing service is an attitude.
Providing service is an action of the heart.
Providing service is positional.
Providing service is operational

What it is not is Lip Service. Make sure your words are being demonstrated through your actions at all times. Leaders are action oriented with performance. When your character speaks louder than your performance, trust is developed which will always bring fruitfulness. The leader and servant will be become a well-known team among others and a model to replicate through faith.

A good leader is always looking for opportunities to bring elevation to those who serve them. Realizing there should always be a protégé being raised up to take the helms of the business. A bad visionary leaves no successor to continue the vision onward. Training is essential for leaders. It is the willingness to share information show maturity and self-confidence that the business can still go forth without their presence. If a leader feels their business cannot run without them keep training for growth is not your portion, at least not at this time. Stop looking at the flesh of your leader and look deeper at their heart. You will be surprised at what you see.

Chapter Seven
Start Over

What is so exuberant about life is, Start Over's. No matter where you are in your life right now and if you are not pleased with it, you can start over. File a mental bankruptcy with yourself. Get a clean visual slate in your mind and begin to think about your future. Construct a business plan concerning your life. Where there is no plan, there is need for ordering of steps.

If you have not done well in your servitude, start over. Improve your customer service skills. Work on you. Come up with the worst-case scenario and fix a response in your mind. Rehearse it, so that when a challenge comes you can pass the test.

Most places of employment do a Personality Assessment. Where they ask multiple questions concerning your character/personality and your replies will be shown through the answers you provide. This will determine if you are a good fit for the company.

There is nothing wrong in not accepting a servitude position, especially if you know you are not suitable for that leader. Do not let anyone make you feel guilty or less humane about saving your leader and yourself from some heartache that could develop along the way. It is important to be true to oneself at all costs.

I recall being offered a position that I refused and I politely informed my superior (after being asked why); we don't get along well as colleagues and it is only setting us both up to fail. I respected her in order to be honest with her and she did not deny it. I made the right decision. She liked my skills and ability to perform, but our personalities were no match for each other. Your leader and you will have to be mature to comprehend this, so that offense does not rise up with pride.

Mess-ups happen every single day. Missing the mark occurs more frequently than hitting the mark. Some people don't even see the mark. This is why do-overs are for both leaders and servants. Living in a society where you talk more to machines than humans has diminished our customer service skills of hearing live voices.

Rather than talking, social media has become our way of communicating and interviewing skills are horrible because people do not know how to talk or write. This is why so much miscommunication is on the rise and relationships have been destroyed. Okay people we must start again. Use your voice, again!

We must take the time to talk to each other. Speak words. Listen and respond with verbal speech. I cannot tell you how many times my Corporate Leaders and Spiritual Leaders have misinterpreted the tone of my message in text. I literally had to pick up a phone and clear up the misunderstanding before I was fired or rebuked. Please take note, I had to pick up the phone. Humility is of the essence here, not who is right or wrong. Please take heed servants across the land.

Your assignment is this:
- Correct what has been wronged in your servitude toward your leaders today
- Bring the Joy back in Serving
- Practice your responses
- Smile even when you do not feel like it
- Be available

- Get control of you own C.U.P.

Get It Together

There was a disciple by the name of Peter who walked with Jesus the totality of his three year ministry. He received much impartation from his leader along with teaching and demonstration. One day the leader was taken away to be placed into jail which happens even in our society today. Jesus twelve men crew was disturbed in seeing this evolve before their eyes that they dispersed themselves with each one going in their own direction. It was not a good time to be associated with Jesus, the leader.

While Jesus was in jail, members of society recognized Peter as being one of Jesus' followers. When asked the question was he Jesus' disciple, Peter instantly denied that he ever knew the man. This kind of reaction is usually common when a leader is removed in this kind of manner. Don't point fingers or judge. Peter denied his leader three times, one for each year he followed. (Luke 22:56-61)

As servants, can you remain in position in the absence of your Leader? Only you can answer this important question. Peter felt bitterly sorrowful for his actions. How could he deny the man who taught him so much and believed in his service? Yet it happens more than I care to say. Leaders feel betrayed by those who serve them and this causes a breach of trust. Having the ability to reconcile (restore) is a healing process that works if the two agree. (II Cor. 5:18)

Jesus (the leader) did not forget Peter and he forgave him. Before his denial occurred, Jesus prepared his servant by saying, *"But I have prayed for thee, that thy faith fail not: and when thou art converted, strengthen thy brethren but I have prayed especially for you Peter, that your faith and confidence in Me may not fail; and you, once you have turned back again to Me, strengthen and support your brothers in the faith."* (Luke 22:32) Peter was blessed with a start over before he even messed up and given a new assignment; "Strengthen the Brethren". Your failures allow room for strength to be developed. It is a witness of your weakness.

Peter became one of the greatest students, mentee, disciple, apostle. He learned to forgive himself. Your servitude can be the greatest honor to your leader as you too become what you are purposed to be. You have been graced to start over and this time you will succeed in being the servant you were designed to be until your partnership comes into effect.

I want to personally say, CONGRATULATIONS on your new assignment! It awaits you.

Be blessed and I want to ask again, "Are There Any Minions In The House?" The correct response should be "YES THERE ARE!"

Practice Makes Perfect
30 Day Challenge

To become better servers you have to practice. Below you are being provided a task to perform. This is to help you get to a place of security in your serving.

Day One
Provide Your Definition of Servant

_____
_____
_____
_____
_____
_____
_____
_____
_____
_____

Day Two
Provide Your Definition of Leader

_____
_____
_____
_____
_____
_____
_____
_____

Day Three
Define Your Relationship with Your Leader

_____
_____
_____
_____
_____
_____
_____
_____

Day Four
List how Your Leader has Challenged You

_____
_____
_____
_____
_____
_____
_____
_____

Day Five
List what You need to Improve about Yourself and Do It

_____
_____
_____
_____
_____
_____
_____
_____

Day Six
Create A Servant Resume

_____
_____
_____
_____
_____
_____
_____

Day Seven
Work on Patience Today
With Yourself and Your Leader

_____
_____
_____
_____
_____
_____
_____

Day Eight
Check Your Hearing on Today
In addition, the Interpretation of What You Hear

_____
_____
_____
_____
_____
_____
_____
_____

Day Nine
Describe Your
Weaknesses and Strengths

_____
_____
_____
_____
_____
_____
_____
_____

Day Ten
Your Response to ALL Requests is OKAY

Day Eleven
Think Yourself Happy

Day Twelve
Love Unconditionally

_____
_____
_____
_____
_____
_____
_____

Day Thirteen
Focus on Your Stamina of Keeping Up

_____
_____
_____
_____
_____
_____
_____
_____

Day Fourteen
Study to Be Quiet

Day Fifteen
Be the Solution to the Problem

Day Sixteen
How are You C.U.P.ing Your Position

Day Seventeen
If You were Graded
Would You Pass or Fail

Day Eighteen
Don't be M.I.A.
Gather Yourself, but Return

_____

_____

_____

_____

_____

_____

_____

Day Nineteen
Accomplish the Task that has been Requested Ahead of Schedule

_____

_____

_____

_____

_____

_____

_____

Day Twenty
Ask Your Questions in Private

_____
_____
_____
_____
_____
_____
_____

Day Twenty - One
Show Unity with Your leader

_____
_____
_____
_____
_____
_____
_____

Day Twenty - Two
Never Allow Anyone to Talk about Your Leader Especially You

_____
_____
_____
_____
_____
_____
_____
_____

Day Twenty-Three
Be Able to Keep Secrets

_____
_____
_____
_____
_____
_____
_____
_____

Day Twenty-Four
Watch Attitude in Taking Orders

Day Twenty-Five
Look at Your Hands and Pray they Cause No Harm

Day Twenty-Six
Thank Your Leader for The Opportunity to Serve them

_____
_____
_____
_____
_____
_____
_____

Day Twenty-Seven
Your Leader offers what style of Love towards You: Influence, Resources, Humility

_____
_____
_____
_____
_____
_____
_____

Twenty-Eight
Give Your Leader a Compliment In Person not on the Phone

_____
_____
_____
_____
_____
_____
_____
_____

Day Twenty-Nine
Does Your Dress Style Compliment Your Leader

_____
_____
_____
_____
_____
_____
_____
_____

Day Thirty
What Is Your Leader's Vision?

Servitude Resume References

Jesus was the epitome of a "Servant Leader"! When he walked the earth, he fed the hungry and he washed the feet of his disciples!

Jesus did not come to be served but he came to serve! Every week I watch to see who among our leadership will be the greatest today! It is not the one who will preach the best or the one that will release the most profound prophetic word but it will be the one that shows up with "their towel" that will translate as some service to God's people! Truly, the greatest among us is the one who chooses to serve!

I am happy to say as the Senior Leader of The Empowerment Word & Truth Church that my daughter Monica Lloyd "chooses" to serve the house every week, therefore I see her as great!

Apostle Robbie C. Peters
One of the NOT MANY Fathers

Servitude Resume References

SERVICE is something you render to another! A SERVANT is someone who serves another and as it relates to the kingdom, it is the way greatness is exhibited! Upon your arrival to glory, your Heavenly Father wants to greet you with these words, "WELL DONE THY GOOD AND FAITHFUL SERVANT".

I am happy to say that I could send God an email reference today and say, "Dear Lord, I'm happy to report that Pastor Monica Lloyd has done well as a servant, and Lord she yet remains faithful. So please Sir, count her amongst the great ones in your kingdom"!

Lovingly Submitted,
Apostle Mom, Sharon Peters

ABOUT THE AUTHOR

Executive Pastor Monica D. Lloyd is a woman with an Apostolic Teaching Anointing, who is able to discern the Intents of the Heart of Mankind and bring them into Deliverance through her teachings with clarity of God's Word to the Body of Christ. She is purposed to live life on purpose, as she goes forth feeding the nations.

Being in ministry for many years, she has discovered that serving others is a "Kingdom Necessity" for growth and development in the things of Christ, which makes her an Invested Commodity toward the building of the Kingdom of God. Leaving ones selfish desires along with self-willed ambitions will allow for maturation and one walking into the purposes, plans, and destiny of God.

Pastor Monica, as she is affectionately called by the congregation of The Empowerment Word & Truth Church, serves under the auspicious guiding of Senior Leadership of the Apostles Robbie C Peters & Sharon R. Peters. She believes being planted in the right church home will develop believers into becoming the model church of maturation. Pastor Monica also serves as a Board of Director for Sweet Rose of Sharon Women's Ministry. A ministry determined to teach, train, strengthen and support women while bringing about healing and restoration through the Word of God to women everywhere.

Pastor Monica uses her first ministry, which is Evangelism, to share with others that having a relationship with Jesus Christ will bring about a life changing experience, which will manifest into the "New Man" described in II Corinthians 5:17. No one can come to Christ and expect to be the same!

Working since the age of 15 has taught her valuables lessons of serving others. It's not so much positional as it is an attitude of performance. Serving others is a matter of the heart.

Pastor Monica is the wife of a loving and supportive husband of 29 years, Elder, Sir George Lloyd and the mother of three wonderful sons, Cory, Louis and Julian. She is an anointed speaker, contributing writer for EMagazine, Kingdom Exec., has written several articles, newsletters, etc. and is the author of the book "7 Things A Woman Needs To Know", "Living Life On Purpose" and "Are There Any Minions In The House ~ Better Understanding Your

Service". Her motto in life is "I Am Living Kingdom In Style".

Monica D Lloyd
Kingdomperspective13@gmail.com
Facebook: Monica Lloyd
Twitter: @MonicaDLloydDD
Instagram: monicalloyd12

www.ingramcontent.com/pod-product-compliance
Lightning Source LLC
LaVergne TN
LVHW051509070426
835507LV00022B/3009